the joy of being online
all the f*cking time

the art of losing your mind*

*literally

jennifer mccartney

the countryman press
an imprint of w. w. norton & company
independent publishers since 1928

For information about permission to reproduce selections
from this book, write to Permissions, The Countryman Press,
500 Fifth Avenue, New York, NY 10110

For information about special discounts for bulk purchases,
please contact W. W. Norton Special Sales at
specialsales@wwnorton.com or 800-233-4830

Manufacturing by LSC Communications, North Harrisonburg
Book design by Nick Caruso
Production manager: Gwen Cullen

The Countryman Press
www.countrymanpress.com

A division of W. W. Norton & Company, Inc.
500 Fifth Avenue, New York, NY 10110
www.wwnorton.com

978-1-68268-465-8

10 9 8 7 6 5 4 3 2 1

"The internet, man, is a beautiful thing."

—THE WEEKND

"The internet's completely over."

—PRINCE

do not disturb

off

Introduction

"I enjoy being active, but I look forward
to the day when I can retire to the internet."

—DANIEL KAHNEMAN

network of ♡

You're online. All the fucking time. We all are.

And why not? Being online is wonderful and revolutionary and easy: your phone, your laptop, your desktop, your tablets, your e-readers and smartwatches, and loveable family robot servants are all plugged into the global interconnected network we know and love as "the internet." This glorious place gives us access to essential information, enabling us to all be extremely smart. Who needs a PhD when the web allows us answers to things like When can we lick subway poles again? What is the outdoors? Who is Meghan Markle? (the most searched person after she and Harry got engaged, after which she subsequently moved to California in what's possibly the biggest fuck-you to the Royal Family since Royal Family fuckery began), or gives us info on "Baby Yoda" (the most searched "baby" of its year, followed by "Baby Shark"). If fashion is your thing, instructions on how to dress like an e-girl or e-boy are readily available (a top fashion search when everyone decided to dress like it was 1994 again.)* Also a popular search: Will they know if I'm not wearing pants to my video confrence?

You'd never know, would you? Without the internet you might not even wonder about these things. Not only are you learning, you're becoming more curious every time you tap out one of your questions. It's mind expanding.

The ability to be online is fucking insane. It's delightful. All of humanity and every single

....

* This is bafflingly described as "electronic, Internet Explorer logo in vaporwave style," which, whatever the fuck. It's like a Hot Topic store mixed with Sailor Moon and pastels, if that means anything to you. If you already know about this, it's because of the internet, so congratulations.

technological discovery and intelligent thought that came before us in history has led to this moment. Screens—first on our desktops, then laptops, then phones—are a portal into infinity and immortality and knowledge and acceptance. It's space big enough for everyone, where you and your friends and the algorithms slowly learning everything about you can exist in peace and connectivity.

If you're reading this book, you probably already know that some folks—hand-wringing, anti-fun, anti-technology crusaders—see the internet as an evil, humanity-sucking entity that is turning all of us into mindless, self-centered, immoral bullies who watch porn and cyberstalk our enemies. That shit does happen and it's bad. But the goodness outweighs the bad by a million tons of elephants. Thank you, pandemic. Screens have won. We've all had a crash course in digital maximalism now and there's no turning back. You know this. Yet sometimes we doubt ourselves. That's where this book comes in: to save you from the bullshit "digital detoxing" crowd. To save you from their fucking tedious bullshit. To help you open up to the internet, and allow it to become one with your soul.

"The bottom line is, the brain is wired to adapt."

—STEVEN YANTIS,
PROFESSOR OF PSYCHOLOGICAL
AND BRAIN SCIENCES,
JOHNS HOPKINS UNIVERSITY

Here's my take: No matter what fucking things we do to our brains, our brains figure it out. That's why the dude you went to high school with who'd wake and bake every morning and hotbox his car every lunch hour and go to raves on weekends is now a successful investment banker and owns a house and pool where he gets drunk on sunny weekends. His brain didn't let him down. And yours won't either. Probably. People who use the internet are more efficient at finding information, according to brain imaging scans. Some of us even have higher levels of brain activity than those who prefer to get their information from crystals or something. We're all geniuses.

BLAH, BLAH, BLAH

....

"Is the internet killing our brains?" asks *The Guardian*. "Is the internet bad for us?" asks the BBC. "Attached to technology and paying a price," warns the *New York Times*. Not to mention the articles and books with judgy titles like *Put Down Your Fucking Phone, How to Digital Detox, Stop Scrolling, Start Living,* and my favorite, *Amazing Secrets of Digital Minimalism*. Is "digital maximalism" the real reason that we're all becoming unfeeling, distracted people unable to focus on one task or on our relationships? Is the internet killing our appetite for sex? For encouraging meaningless arguments with strangers?

The internet destroys our brains and also society, the argument goes. In fact, teen pregnancy rates are at their lowest levels since 1957 (the Pew Research Center suggests one reason is that teens are having less sex. The internet says you're welcome). Teen drug use of all kinds is also at its lowest level since 2004, according to the National Institute for Drug Abuse for Teens, while alcohol use is also way lower than its peak in the late 1990s—right around the time many teens got a computer with dial-up internet. Coincidence? Of course not.

So come the fuck on. We have enough to worry about—the climate crisis, the rise of fascism, etc.—without worrying about how often we're online. Yet, apparently this is just one more thing we need to feel guilty about. One more thing for which we need to develop discipline. One more item to add to our self-restraint to-do list.

your brain
on the
internet?

Despite the wonders of the internet, the pressure to "get offline" is so strong that one in four adults has reportedly tried a digital detox. That's bullshit. It's not practical, it's not realistic, and it's setting us up to fail. If you've ever spotted a holier-than-thou quiz like this, you'll know what I mean:

1. Do you check your phone before bed?

2. Do you check your phone when you're feeling bored?

3. Do you find yourself spending time online to avoid real-life interactions?

I mean, what the fuck. Yes.

The idea, however, is that answering yes to any of these questions means you've got an issue with your phone or internet use. That you could use a break. That it's time to have a think about how often you're online. When, in fact, answering yes to these questions means you're an average human being who's alive today and existing in the world. And probably doing pretty well, seeing as how you're so well connected and informed. In fact, pat on the back to you, informed internet citizen.

Digital detoxing is for the rich. Who has the time or money to do a five-day, off-the-grid retreat in the Joshua Tree desert, learning to interpret the stars and sunning our vaginas while making hemp belts? I mean, I love doing that stuff, in theory. That sounds relaxing and probably our vaginas like a bit of sun once in awhile, who knows. But who has the luxury of ignoring their emails and texts and social media for hours or days on end? People who don't need to work and who have fantastic personal assistants, even though they don't have jobs and technically shouldn't need an assistant, that's who.

This freaking out is part of a predictable cycle that happens every time some new invention becomes commonplace. Every generation does some hand-wringing about how technology is ruining humanity. A 1907 article in the *New York Times* supported the idea that the telephone inspired rudeness: "The general use of the telephone, instead of promoting civility and courtesy, is the means of the fast dying out of what little we have left." [Insert jerking off emoji here.] Buy a television and radio will become extinct! Motorized carriages will scare the horses! Digital media will kill off print! This is the perfect book for everyone who loves their phone. Go ahead and check your email obsessively while on vacation. Don't feel bad about it. Follow a trending hashtag, read, text, and listen to all manner of shit at all hours. In fact, you should know where your phone is at all times and live online as much as humanely possible, except when you're reading a book (see page 48). Never feel shitty about your internet use! Life is too fucking short for guilt. And the internet is too big and wide and beautiful to waste time socializing with actual people. Go ahead and be online all the fucking time.*

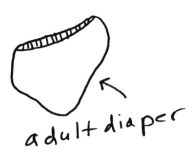

a dult diaper

* Unless of course you have an actual addiction to the internet that's inhibiting your ability to function in society (which still exists, somehow, despite all this tech). If the scales have tipped from normal-person-using-the-internet into something more serious, this book is not for you. Have you ever worn a diaper to aid your nonstop internet use? Yes? Call your doctor and your mother.

disclaimer

The ability to be online all the fucking time is real and it's wonderful and we're all very good at the internet and we don't want to do without it. However. Don't overdo it, you maniac. Just like those who eschew minimalism in favor of stuff run the risk of becoming a hoarder, so those of us who enjoy technology and internet-related things run the risk of becoming addicted to a video game and shitting ourselves and then dying of a heart attack due to too many energy drinks. These are the people on the extreme end of things who, due to addiction or boredom or whatever, find themselves needing help. If that's you, put down this e-book and consult a medical professional.

If you're reading this book to help you better deal with life and your perceived shortcomings, then good for you. Books are great. Life is hard sometimes and also very often full of bullshit. But as I've said before in other anti-self-help books, this book won't fix you or solve your problems.

The best you can hope for is that all this makes you laugh a little bit and reminds you that life is too fucking short for detoxes of any kind—internet included. I mean, they don't work. You know this on some level. Detoxing is nonsense. Diets don't work. Enemas don't work. I'm fairly certain minimalism is meant to make you feel bad about yourself. Live your life however you want. Live it online. It's all good. Your brain will be fine. And if it isn't, what will you care? You'll be living your virtual life—illness-free and debt-free and with your true unicorn self as an avatar and full of interesting info you just googled. Alive.

why i wrote this book:
a lesson in not
trusting your friends

Once upon a time, some friends of ours came to live in our apartment and we went to live in theirs. A flat swap, we called it, because our friends were British and the English have the best words for everything. We did this because we were young and had no children, and it seemed like a fun and economical way to spend a few weeks. They came to Brooklyn and we went to London. It was an inexpensive vacation while still requiring you to do the dishes and the laundry, which keeps you from enjoying yourself too much. We arrived late at night and opened the bottle of wine they'd kindly left us. The next day I messaged my friend asking about the wi-fi password. Oh, he wrote. This is a bit awkward. We cancelled our internet a few months ago. We're trying to be online less.

That is a shitty thing to discover, as you might imagine, if you're like me and spend every second online and if you go to sleep with your phone on your pillow. Or if you use the internet for work, which I do. What. The. Fuck.

This was back when cell phone companies charged for international data, which meant using my cell phone to get online was prohibitively expensive. I know this because at one point, my partner gave in and uploaded a photo of his fish and chips to social media and he was charged $300. A dollar for every megabyte or some sort of corporate thievery. Tax the corporations, by the way. Tax them all.

I considered my options. There were no trendy coffee shops nearby where one could hang out and do work. But there were some neighborhood pubs that opened around noon. So every morning I'd head a few doors down to the Swan and Beaver,* buy a pint of cider, and make it last as long as possible while I got some work done. Cider feels like a day drink, doesn't it? It's basically apple juice. Sometimes, if the gods were with me, I could get the bar's wi-fi signal from the flat's front stoop. So I'd hunch there furtively for hours with my laptop, sending emails and checking on world events while normal internet-having people walked their dogs and went about their day, fully connected.

The point is that my friend had fallen prey to the "scientific, peer-reviewed studies by award-winning scientists" out there dictating how bad the internet actually is for your human brain or your memory, and he and I are

---

* A fun game is to think of two unrelated nouns and then look up how many pubs in England actually have that name. Fox and Coxswain. Apple and Grouse. Hat and Staircase. Etc.

still friends but we occasionally talk about what a dick move that was on his part, even though I pretended everything was fine and waited ten years to put the incident in this book. Anyway, people need the internet. That's a fact of modern life. And I was kind of fucking pissed that my friend did not have it. Our evenings were spent in the back garden with a bottle of wine, birdsong in our ears, bitching about the nerve of our friends. Miserable.

1.

What God Hath Wrought

"I was pretty tired when I made that comment because I had been up very late the night before inventing the camcorder."

—AL GORE,[*]

REGARDING HIS COMMENT ABOUT INVENTING THE

INTERNET

....

[*] Al Gore did not invent the camcorder.

A brief history of the interwebs

Maybe you already know how to code and understand that the internet is made up of a series of tubes. Or perhaps you just know how to turn your phone on and scroll. Regardless of your internet understanding, here's a brief primer so we're all on the same page.

The early internet made its appearance in the '60s as ARPANET (the Advanced Research Projects Agency Network), thanks to funding by the US Department of Defense. The idea was, we needed a way to share information quickly and over great distances, and also this was during the Cold War and everyone was afraid the Russians would beat us at this technology thing. Guess who got the last laugh! Anyway, the initial goal was "time-sharing." Where one computer and the information it contained could be used by many users at the same time. The first successful ARPANET message was sent between researchers at Stanford and UCLA in 1969.

ARPANET

"We set up a telephone connection between us and the guys at SRI," said UCLA computer scientist Leonard Kleinrock in an interview. "We typed the L and we asked on the phone,

'Do you see the L?'

'Yes, we see the L.'

We typed the O, and we asked, 'Do you see the O.'

'Yes, we see the O.'

Then we typed the G, and the system crashed."

And there you have it. The illustrious beginnings of the world's craziest invention. A thing so advanced it was unable to handle the letter G. Instead of "login," possibly the nerdiest word they could have chosen, the world's first internet message was "lo." The first message sent by Sam Morse via telegraph? "What God hath wrought." If you're interested, the computer lab where this happened is now a little museum. If you like looking at hulking chunks of outdated technology and 1960s furniture, definitely check it out.

During the 1970s, more engineers worked on building the internet, and in the 1980s, the military dropped out from its role in research (see: "lo," above) and the National Science Foundation took over. In the early '90s, Al Gore sponsored the High Performance Computing Act, which paved the way for the information superhighway and his infamous comment nearly a decade later: "I took the initiative in creating the internet." In 1994, Bill Clinton turned over control of "the internet backbone" to the people, where it's been ever since. The internet is not "owned" by anyone—technically, anyone who wants to connect can go for it. Unless you live in North Korea.

"Turn On, Boot Up, Jack IN"

The internet was well on its way to becoming a cool punk thing. In fact, famous Harvard psychologist and LSD lover Timothy Leary proclaimed that the "PC* is the LSD of the 1990s," encouraging everyone to embrace a new cyberdelic culture. That we "turn on, boot up, jack in." As anyone who has seen the '90s film *Hackers* can attest, early cyberculture was very cool and also very antiestablishment. If the movies and books about this era are to be believed, everyone was gender fluid, incredibly smart, and prepared to use their special hacking skills to take on criminal enterprise, corrupt governments, and evil corporations. Their attire usually involved lots of leather and a pair of rollerblades. It makes sense that someone like Leary was interested in the internet's myriad possibilities—he wanted us to expand our minds by any means possible. The internet was one way to do that.** I'm sure he'd

---

* A PC is a personal computer. It's sort of like your phone, only way bigger.

** Also, drugs.

be happy to know we're all literally turned on and jacked into everything these days.[*]

So join me, will you, as we turn to the BYTE ME Manifesto. This is the real counterculture movement. This is your brave new world. This will help you reach a higher level of consciousness.[**]

John Lennon

....

[*] Fun fact: John Lennon wrote "Come Together" as a campaign song for Timothy Leary's failed run to be the governor of California.

[**] No. Drugs might, though. Leary was right about that.

BYTE ME!

The BYTE ME Manifesto

"The ultimate promise of technology is to make us master of a world that we command by the push of a button."

—VOLKER GRASSMUCK

The BYTE ME Manifesto will help you maximize your online experiences. You have so much potential. The BYTE ME Manifesto is here to help you be the best digital maximalist you can be.

Repeat after me: I am a global citizen of the twenty-second century. Or is it the twenty-first? There's so much misinformation online now and my critical thinking skills aren't super developed. Whatever. Irrelevant! I use electricity and the telephone and the internet and, shortly, probably, flying electric bicycles that pilot themselves. My quality of life and my brain power are vastly superior to those born in the pre-internet age. I embrace the tenets of digital maximalism. Here are the rules I live by:

Be online, always. Never turn anything off, ever. You never know when you'll feel bored for a fraction of a second. Or need to take a photo of a beautiful apple that looks like Celine Dion.

Yell at everyone online in a measured way, offering an informed or uninformed opinion about everything. Share every thought about current events, as it occurs to you, with everyone, regardless of whether or not it involves you in any way. A celebrity likes olives? You fucking love olives. Tell them! Be sure to do this using whatever online persona you want. There's no need to reveal your real name.

Take a moment to appreciate how fucking lucky you are to have the goddamn internet. Do it right now, you ungrateful piece of shit. We're encouraged to view our online life as a bad thing. It's not. It's beautiful. Let go of that toxic, anti-tech energy and embrace gratitude. Download a gratitude app, if it helps.

End the tyranny of answering your phone. If for some reason someone calls you on the telephone like an old-timey person, let it go to voicemail. When you get around to listening to that voicemail from three months ago, reply with a text that says something like, hey, sorry to not reply sooner but you called me like a complete dick and listening to my voicemails is actually kind of a hassle. And sorry I missed the funeral.

Meeting in person is inefficient—don't do it. A digital maximalist never calls or meets in person if they can achieve the same results online. Meetings, check-ins, birthday parties. This also helps keep you healthy. Other people are very germy. Also you can drink all day at home and no one is the wiser. Not even the CEO you just video conferenced with.

Evaluate whether or not a task could be done online. Parenting. School. Heart surgery. Watercolors. Whatever it is. If the answer is yes, do it online.

what's your technology love language?

Take this definitely scientifically backed quiz to find out.

1. What's the best, most recent tech invention?

A. The zipper.

B. An app for ordering the latest limited-edition shrimp-mayo-flavored Doritos and Peach Coke from Japan.

C. Cryonics—I'm going to have my body filled with antifreeze and preserved in a pod inside an Arizona cryonics facility after I die. 2188, here I come!

2. When it comes to road trips, what's your get-there strategy?

A. Cars are for assholes. I ride my bicycle everywhere. It's made of sustainable bamboo and melted glacier water.

B. GPS. How the fuck else do you get anywhere?

C. My car is named Christine. She's an excellent navigator and her seats vibrate. I'm so lonely.

3. Temperature control is a necessary luxury because the planet is overheating and we're all going to die. When it comes to making sure you're not living in a sweatbox, your strategy is:

A. My cabin is in a remote northern location and built with geothermal techniques that make it naturally cooling. However, when I do get too hot, I meditate on how all of humanity deserves to die a fiery death;

B. Automated thermostat controlled by an app;

C. The rooms in my tropical island estate are all set to a cool 66 degrees, which is the temperature at which the body burns the most calories, according to science.

4. If you died watching your favorite TV program* and the undertakers wanted to turn off the TV before removing the body, how easy would that be?

....

* Wouldn't that be a nice way to go? Drifting off to the underworld with the sound of Michael Scott in your ears?

A. I don't own a television. Trees are my must-watch TV. And oh so bingeable.

B. There are two remotes—one for the streaming thing and the other for the actual TV. They should be able to figure it out.

C. My entertainment system is controlled by a wireless chip in my hand. Good luck operating it without the correct biometrics, asshole.

Answer Key:

Mostly As: The frigid lover. You're a bit of a Luddite. There's nothing overly wrong with that. The history of Luddites is actually very cool and radical. In the 1800s, a loosely organized group of workers began to protest the introduction of automated textile equipment in factories across England. They worried this new technology (and the cheap labor it brought with it) threatened their jobs. Sound familiar? The Luddites destroyed a few knitting and lace-making machines in protest, and even killed a mill owner, before the British army got involved. Soon after, the government made it a capital crime to destroy a machine. Wild, right? Anyway, you're probably more chill about technology than the actual Luddites and don't go around smashing electric scooters and automated kiosks in protest. But technology can also make your life easier—it wouldn't hurt to reevaluate its role in your life.

Luddite

Mostly Bs: The warm consensual hug. You've got a solid relationship with technology. You acknowledge what it can do for you and how it can make your life easier. See how great tech can be? You're not wandering around feeling guilty for owning zippers or having an email account.

Mostly Cs: Codependent and polyamorous. You can't live without all the latest shit. You love tech and you're probably also rich because new tech is expensive. You're also probably reading this book on your smartwatch. Or perhaps your robot butler is reading it for you. Anyway, tech is great, but you may be overdoing it. When's the last time you spoke with a person in the flesh and in the daylight?*

----

* No, not a Fleshlight. Those don't count.

A special note about phones

When we say "online," what we really mean is "on our phones." And by "phones," we mean "smartphones." Phones keep getting better and better. Back in the day when everything was in black and white and people still wrote letters and died from measles, giant plastic phones or "landlines" were plugged into the wall phone socket, and the phone receiver was connected to the phone base with a cord. If you wanted privacy, you had to pull the phone base as far as it would go toward, say, your teenage bedroom, and then stretch the cord as far as that would go, and then shut your door to whisper to your bestie how Todd was a dreamboat and that you'd fucked. Now you can literally be jogging in a forest and still send your bestie an eggplant and a dancing vulva superimposed over a screenshot of Todd's face, and she totally gets the message. Thanks, smartphones!

A PHONE APPRECIATION
EXERCISE FOR PEOPLE WHO LIKE
THIS SORT OF THING

....

*"As a form of escapism, yearning for the 20th
century is understandable, but in practice
it would be horrible—sort of like going on a
holiday promising yourself you could go
without the internet, only to crumble and
walk in a daze to the local internet café to
gorge on connectivity."*

—DOUGLAS COUPLAND

We can't learn to love ourselves and our internet
use without first loving the vehicle of progress
that has brought it to our fingertips. This is a
mindfulness lesson in loving your phone. Many
of us associate mindfulness with activities like
goat yoga or drinking moringa tea sprinkled with
bee pollen or living in an off-the-grid converted

bus in northern Australia.* However, mindfulness can apply to technology, as well. We can set our intentions and close our eyes and give thanks to just about anything. Chocolate chunk cookies? Gratitude. A pair of fluffy slippers made of bunny skin? Gratitude. A seat at the bar that's far from the service area and not behind the draft taps? Gratitude. So here's a mindfulness exercise in cultivating gratitude that will help you embrace the very sexy, very healthy, and not codependent relationship between you and your phone.

Set your phone on a flat surface where you can see it. Concentrate on your phone. Think about what you love about it. Perhaps it's your phone's ability to connect you with friends and family or its excellent photo-taking abilities. Perhaps it's the way it makes you feel less alone. Now close your eyes, and send these feelings of appreciation to your phone. Send it all the love,

* There are currently forty-five social media influencers who fit this exact description, probably.

and thankfulness, and good vibes. Send it all the soft-cloud energy you usually reserve for Labradors or koalas drinking bottled water.* Tell it, silently, what you love about it and how much it means to you. In fact, give it a name, if you want. Frank. Lois. Archie. Steven. Whatever feels right. Now, open your eyes. Pick up your phone and run your fingers around the edges. Feel the curves and notice if there's any debris or smudges that need your attention. How can you help the phone look its best? How can you show it respect? Gently clean the screen until it shines. Now, wake it up, gently. Observe the home screen or lock screen and think about how many times you see this image in a day. Probably around 68 times according to some uptight study that says we look at our phones too much. And

----

* Because of all the forest fires in Australia. The parched koalas can't find enough water and they approach humans for help. Humans give them water and transport them to animal shelters, and these sweet videos are another reason no one should ever talk shit about the internet.

feel grateful for this image. For what it represents. The portal to infinity and immortality and friendship. You and your phone are one—inseparable. It knows your secrets. It knows which categories of porn inspire you. It's aware of which ex-partner you revisit and search for and agonize over, even though they always lied about their height and are married now to a woman who sells leggings online. It knows which pair of booties you want but can't afford. It's with you in your lowest moments, your highest highs. It is you and you are it. Accepting this, truly knowing this in the deepest bits of your human organs that will also probably be replaced at some point by artificial organs that connect to the internet, is the first step in learning to love being online, all the fucking time.

phone from the
past

A special note about books

"I got into trouble a while ago for saying that I thought the internet led to increased literacy— people scolded me about the shocking grammar to be found online—but I was talking about fundamentals: quite simply, you can't use the net unless you can read."

—MARGARET ATWOOD

Books are one of those things science can't improve upon. They are perfect artifacts and have maintained the same form for centuries because they're already the best they can be. Paper is a magical thing, and ink and words are not to be fucked with. Reading books is an analog joy and the one exception to this entire book, which obviously you already know because you're reading a book and not streaming something right now. Unless this is an audiobook or an e-book, in which case [insert slow clap noise here]. Anyway, buy your books in person at a bookstore. Book people are wonderful and bookstores are one of the last magical places in the world, and we should all be grateful for them.

2.

Lose Your Mind Online

"In this electric age we see ourselves being translated more and more into the form of information, moving toward the technological extension of consciousness."

—MARSHALL MCLUHAN

your brain
online

Get ready to forget everything . . . and become the smartest person you know. Because looking at our phone is hard on our short-term memory and increases what fancy neuro people call our "cognitive load." It appears, according to science, that using our phones can inhibit our ability to remember things. Which is . . . I forget. But the good news is that you don't need to remember. Just google it. Your brain is the internet now. Remembering is for suckers. Everything you need to know is online—your learning happens in real time and retention isn't necessary. Of course, the internet isn't just for learning. It's also the best place to go to literally not think about or learn

51

anything ever. The most effective way to quickly lose your mind is probably the new dancing app where teenagers all do the same dance to the same song in slightly different ways in a shockingly weird display of homogenous conformity, but whatever, millions of views. Followed by YouTube* and Netflix, and any site with respectful celebrity gossip (not the weird stalker kind with photos of them and their children).

Bury the pain of reality with the New Reality

Forgetting shit has other benefits, too. The world is mean and terrible, with weather that makes it hard to go outside and news that makes it hard to want to wake up. Want to avoid your bad relationship? Ignore a global pandemic? Difficult classes? Annoying-as-fuck children? Go online.

....

* Actually watching tutorials is the bomb. You learn a ton of shit you can immediately forget, but it's a great place to spend five hours learning to make your face look like a tiger.

Your dog just stepped really hard on your boob. The spoon is too far away from where you're lying. Looking at your phone allows you a little escape from all that. In fact, it offers you a way to forget. About life. Plug in to unplug. And forget what you came here for. Why are you looking at your phone? What'd you pick it up for, anyway? To aid in the forgetting. So unlock that little bit of magic, your best friend, your oracle, your source of all distraction, this gift of escape. Overload your short-term memory. Fill it with baby alpaca videos and eyeshadow tutorials and texts from friends. Pure bliss. Forget what you came for. And learn something interesting about making udon soup. That's the whole point.

EVENTS MADE BEARABLE BY SMART-PHONES:

1. Weddings

2. Funerals

3. Kids' birthday parties. Unless there's booze, these are never fun. Retreat to sidelines and scroll.

4. The dentist

5. Dating. Especially that part of dinner when you're finished and waiting for the check.

6. Commuting

7. Bad television. More screens are always the answer if your primary screen isn't cutting it.

8. Boring sports events. Oh, look, that other guy has the ball now! No, thank you.

"Often I would catch myself examining a stranger's acai bowl; or watching frantic videos of abdominal routines that I lacked the core muscles to imitate; or zooming in on a photograph of a wine cellar in Aspen; or watching a serial video of hands assembling a tiny, intricate bowl of udon noodle soup. My brain had become a trash vortex, representations upon representations. Then again, I hadn't known what a wine cellar was supposed to look like."

—ANNA WIENER, *UNCANNY VALLEY*

Digital Maximalist Tip

Check your phone as many times a day
as you feel like. If it's less than 68 times,
you're doing it wrong.

Reddit is the people's palace. It's the site we deserve. It's the American Legion and the local church basement and annual small-town parade and the thing that brings people together now that people don't actually get together. If you go on the Brooklyn subreddit, you'll find tourists asking whether Park Slope is safe or what's the best thing to do in Williamsburg, followed by sarcastic responses because everyone in NYC is a dick. Or, they used to be, before everyone in NYC was from Ohio. All welcome! If you go on the Singapore subreddit, you'll find super lovely, educated people debating small points of public transport etiquette, complaints about rude aunties and the National Service, and photos of sunsets. It's all moderated, so it's got a simulacrum of respectability and civility. And it's where we can all go to ask things like, "Did anyone hear that loud bang followed by a flash of light by Sunset Park?" and get responses like, "Yeah, I heard it too" and "Anyone down to hang out, I recently moved here from Ohio and I feel so, so alone." It's where we can go to find out "Am I the asshole?" and get a resounding yes. Thanks, internet!

internet

A REDDIT POST NOT TAKEN*

....

Two Reddit posts diverged in a yellow wood,
And sorry I could not click on both
And be one internet user, with my
    battery at 2%, long I stood
And scrolled down one as far as I could
To where it bent in the undergrowth;

Then clicked the other, as just as fair,
And having perhaps the better claim,
Because it was trending and I wanted new clothes to wear;
Though as for that the passing there
Had worn them really about the same,
And both that morning equally lay
A comments section no step had trodden black.
Oh, I kept the first for another day!
Yet knowing how my phone charger was far away,
I doubted if I should ever come back.

I shall be telling this with a sigh
Somewhere ages and ages hence:
Two Reddit posts diverged in a wood, and I—
I took the one less traveled by,
And that has made all the difference.

....

* "Check out this major zit I just popped TW extreme
gross" vs. "Check out my Fashion Nova favorites"

YOU CAN WATCH TELEVISION ANYTIME, ANYWHERE!

....

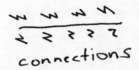

connections

When I was growing up, if you wanted to be entertained, you'd first consult the *TV Guide*. You'd find the current day and time and see what was on offer. Or you'd circle the shit you wanted to watch in the future. Then you'd sit in front of some gigantic thing that weighed four hundred tons and rejoice when remotes were finally invented. Fuck, that was ages ago, and so, so shit, right?

Nowadays, there's no excuse for having cable or even a real TV, honestly. Everything you want and need is available online via any number of streaming services, and it's all portable thanks to your phones and laptops. You don't even need a connection to the internet, as it's easy to download and watch, even when you're on a fucking airplane in the sky. Or perhaps you already know this. A new report by the Nielsen Company found that American adults spend about 10 hours and 39 minutes each day consuming media. This is, really, shameful, and I know we can all do better. Aim for a few more minutes each day—try and bump up that media consumption to eleven hours, or even twelve! Why not? There's so much shit to watch, honestly. Everything is good. TV is amazing. There are fourteen shows you need to catch up on just to be able to chat intelligently with your friends during your next text session. And luckily, thanks to the internet, you can. You just need to put in a little bit of effort.

There are loads of obscure TV shows now available to anyone with time on their hands, or who wants to write a thesis about government-funded children's TV shows from Canada in the '80s. Here is a list of those:

Today's Special—about a mannequin that comes to life in a deparment store at night.

Breaker High—featuring a young Ryan Gosling aboard a learning yacht. Canada's Saved by the Bell. Fun fact: Ryan Gosling and Justin Timberlake were childhood roommates in Florida.

Degrassi High—this show was so badass and everyone knows about it because it was on for forty-three years and infamously had an abortion episode that the US refused to air. It aired in Canada and no doubt inspired millions and millions of young girls to get abortions, just like the politicians warned us about.

Mr. Dressup—Canada's Mr. Rogers. And just as sweet.

Polka Dot Door—magic puppets and a giant green giraffe called the Polkaroo.

Are You Afraid of the Dark?—filmed in British Columbia and Montreal, this kids' horror series was seriously fucking scary, and if you watched it, or let the kids you were babysitting watch it, you'd all have nightmares and all the parents involved would be pissed.

The point is that anything you remember from your childhood is now online and available for late-night nostalgia sessions where you fret about the lack of collagen in your skin and wonder what happened to your youth.

Siri and Alexa and Google Home are at your service

You know when you read an anonymous post by a disgruntled personal assistant to the stars and they're always like, ugh god she only likes rattan furniture and seal-skin mittens and every room she enters must be filled with 400 bottles of blue gatorade and 12 dildos? That's us now.

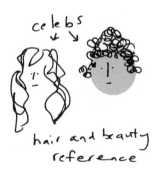

celebs

hair and beauty
reference

With the advent of personal robot assistants, that sort of selfishness on a granular level is now a luxury afforded to all of us. If you'd told me when I was little that I'd be able to say, "Hey Susan, play Celine Dion and also order me some of those ice cream bars that are covered in chocolate and Skittles," and that shit WOULD HAPPEN, I would have told you to go fuck yourself. But it's real now. We live in the future and even the world's least famous citizens can boss robots around. Shopping. Appointment reminders. Music. The weather. Any idiot question you're too embarrassed to ask a real person. What time is it? When's my next parole appointment? How old is my math teacher? Who won the Super Bowl in 1993?

Search bar

You can ask Alexa from the comfort of your car to turn up the heat or turn off the oven. She will tell you jokes and play word games. You can ask how to make a specific cocktail, and she'll order the mixings to arrive on your doorstep within two hours.

Anything you don't know, they know. Anything you need, they've got you. They're listening. So be careful who you murder. Those recordings hold up in court. Your personal assistant is also a snitch.

Outsourcing your brain

One way to lose your mind is to try and do a million things at once. Where better to do that than online? Between your synced-up calendars, personal robot assistants, emails and texts and voice memos, and lightning-quick search capabilities, you're a fucking amazing mix of human and machine, and you deserve some credit. Here it is.

You may be one of the so-called "supertaskers." How do you use the internet? Are you a 300-browser-tabs-open-at-once sort of person? Are you switching back and forth between video, Word documents, email, and those chairs from that store you really love and are waiting to go on sale? Do you somehow manage to get all your work done anyway? Are you also cooking chili and putting on your socks? You may be a supertasker—someone who thrives at multitasking. And you're probably very fucking good at internetting as a result.

About one in forty of us are simply excellent at processing a shit ton of information and can multitask without any issues, both online and off. The University of Utah calls these people supertaskers. A study published in the *Psychonomic Bulletin and Review* found a small part of the population is very good at doing two things at once. The study found these bright little sparks of genius could drive and talk on a cell phone at the same time with no issues, for example.* They could answer math problems and hit the brakes

....

* Dual tasks are nothing for successful internet users. We're doing forty-five things at once. Thanks, brains!

66

simultaneously with no drop in performance in either task. In fact, their memories actually improved by about 3 percent while doing it. I mean, what the fuck. Incredible, right? Now imagine those people online.

"There is clearly something special about the supertaskers," says one of the researchers in an interview. "Why can they do something that most of us cannot? Psychologists may need to rethink what they know about multitasking in light of this new evidence. We may learn from these very rare individuals that the multitasking regions of the brain are different and that there may be a genetic basis for this difference," he says. Supertaskers, the theory goes, can successfully do things like fly fighter jets or date ten people at once or get their homework done while streaming a new show and eating oatmeal. And if you're not one of these supertaskers, perhaps noticing a drop in performance when doing multiple things at once? Literally doesn't matter. Keep at it! Perfection is overrated anyway.

— I'm full!

obsolete file cabinet

cloud storage

Store it all in the cloud

You don't even have to remember where you put anything. Remember when you used to lose things? That won't happen anymore. Before the internet, our music was in physical form. Records, 8-tracks, cassettes, CDs, depending on your age. Or it took up 40,000 megawatts on our hard drive because we had to illegally download it all. Our photos were printed out in albums and stored on bookshelves. Our important papers were in file cabinets stuffed to the brim and difficult to close. We were forced to store real-life shit everywhere and all over. No matter if we lived in a tiny dorm room or one-bedroom apartment. We needed space for all this shit. No longer. Back then, if your house burned down, you were fucked. Now everything we care about is in the cloud. All we ever have to worry about is Russian hackers. Who probably have all your nudes already anyway.* Probably nothing to worry about, unless you decide to run for office one day.

nudes
shared consensually

---

* I assume they teach internet safety as part of every sex-ed class now but just remember never include your face in those nudes you send online. Neck down only, everyone. Plausible deniability if they ever resurface.

what's your internet IQ?

1. How old were you when you got the internet?

A. I've been on social media since my parents posted my ultrasound.

B. I remember our first giant computer with dial-up, and when your parents were on the phone, you couldn't get online, and vice versa. If you were extremely wealthy, you had two phone lines—one for dial-up and one for phone calls. Remember how that spiral phone cord would get all twisted up and you'd have to occasionally unravel it, and then every so often the cord got all stretched out like a middle-aged boob and ended up on the floor?

C. You don't have to "get" the internet. It exists. We are the internet and the internet is us.

2. You sent your first bunny-ear selfie at what age?

   A. 11

   B. 32

   C. That shit is for old people. It's all about gene therapy now. I'm in the process of becoming an actual bunny.

3. You see a bit of paper that needs storing, so you

   A. You mean like a note my friend wrote on actual paper as a joke? I'm not sure I understand the question;

   B. snap a pic but also physically file it, just in case;*

   C. burn it while mumbling a prayer to technology.

....

* When my parents moved out of their house into an apartment, we found a shelf of like a dozen old phone books. This is a perfect example of how things used to be insane and now they're better.

4. The news is information delivered

A. via bite-sized tidbits with accompanying commentary set to a pop song in real time;

B. via my fav media website, which I pay for, because journalism is sacred and we need to support these institutions;

C. into my brain via cochlear implants.

Answer Key:

Mostly As: The internet is a part of life. You're pretty attuned to its latest developments and have grown up learning how to use it responsibly, or not because who actually knows what you're doing online? Not your parents. Your IQ is 130.

Mostly Bs: You remember a time without the internet. You remember your first email address (420420@saturnlink.com). You also probably remember Pogs, Lip Smackers, and being allowed to bicycle without a helmet, because back then nobody cared about kid's brains. You've learned so much since then, but let's face it, you didn't grow up learning how to code. Your IQ is 110.

Mostly Cs: Off the charts. You're from the future. You're so far advanced it's hard for you to relate to our primitive technology. You're likely made of sunshine and inoculated against the flu virus and death. You're immortal and have an organic calculator in your hand.[*] Your intelligence quotient isn't accurately measurable by our antiquated methods.

---

* Growing up, this sort of space-age implant was the height of my and my grade-school chums' idiot imaginations. In the future, we imagined, everyone will have their own calculator. Luxury!

3.

One-Stop Shopping

"People forget already how much utility they get out of the internet—how much utility they get out of email, how much utility they get out of even simple things like brochure-ware* online."

—JEFF BEZOS

....

* Apparently brochureware is when you get a new dishwasher and all the info about how to use it is available online as a handy pdf. I mean, you put dishes in it, and there's a start button, so I guess brochureware is useful if you're some sort of idiot—however, Bezos, lord of the Amazon, is correct about one thing: we tend to forget how much our lives have changed for the better since the advent of the interwebs. But there's always room for improvement.

If you're not using the internet to answer questions you may have about life, chances are you are using it to acquire things. (See my seminal work on buying stuff and leaving it everywhere: *The Joy of Leaving Your Shit All Over the Place*.) You can buy new things, you can buy used things, you can engage in auctions, you can compare prices. You can while away days trying to find the best deals. If you're saving money, you're basically earning money. You can decorate your home, plan a dinner party, and figure out how to fix your dishwasher, all online!

Tuna, coffee tables, eggnog, and yachts

> *"I am not great at computers. If I were to try shopping through Google, I'd end up with 33 vests."*
>
> —MARY BERRY

online Shopping to fill the Void

There's nothing wrong with owning 33 vests if that's what your life's journey dictates. Shopping is a really great way to fill the void until we die. It isn't just frivolous goods we can purchase either—leather pants, a gold cheese knife, a cashmere dog bed—it's the everyday stuff, too. Shopping online makes all of our lives easier. No longer must we go to the general store and put in an order for a bolt of gingham. At least that's what happens in *Anne of Green Gables*, I have no idea. We don't even have to put on underwear, pants, a bra, and a shirt and find our glasses and also the car keys and fuck, I'm tired already. What a huge hassle. It's all online.

A study by Periscope Solutions in 2018 found

that we're all shopping online for everything—around 70 percent of respondents said they'd bought things online, which honestly seems extremely low. One shouldn't lie on surveys. Anyway, stuff like canned goods and beauty products ranked high on the list of stuff we bought often. Which makes sense because canned goods are fucking heavy. Drop that shit at my door, please. I mean, if there was ever an argument for why the internet is amazing, the ability to online shop is fucking IT.

Your bedroom becomes the changing room, you can try stuff on over a period of days at your leisure, and very heavy shit that's a pain to get on your own if you're a weakling and live without a car like me arrives at your door, no problem. Cat litter. Cases of wine. Bags of rice for when the apocalypse comes. Bags of wine. The ability to shop online is also essential for those who aren't able to get out and about easily. That includes parents—even celebrity ones. "Once I had my son," says Solange Knowles, "I stopped shopping in stores because it's not an easy process to try on clothes. . . . I need to do the dance in front of the mirror, the whole nine yards." Relatable!

Shopping online is fast and extremely rewarding. For the credit card companies, mostly. But it's very useful for finding the obscure shit you need from the shops you like, comparison pricing it all, making sure you've taken advantage of all the coupon codes, and then repeating the orders as needed. Roasted garlic and curry ramen? Sure! Maximum Winter Frost–scented mouthwash for men with osteoporosis? Here you go! Size 8¾ tennis shoes with bedazzled ponies? At your door in forty-eight hours.

If you're on the wealthier side of things, order a custom yacht from the comfort of your other custom yacht that's honestly getting a bit dated.*

* I once vacationed in Palm Beach by accident and walked by not one but two yacht stores. Apparently when you order a yacht, you can also order monogrammed china and stuff like that to go with it.

And with apps that shop your local grocery stores, you can still "shop local," support your neighborhood, and enjoy the convenience of not being in an actual fucking shop. Think about how much time you save by not leaving your house to wander around some 50-million-square-foot grocery hall that also does car repairs and sells swimming pools. Please fuck off with the gigantic megastore already. It's like entering a walkathon when you get in there, and those places are depressing as fuck, generally. Ten miles later, you're suffering from a vitamin D deficiency and exhausted and the cart is heavy and now you've got to line up to check out with everyone else in your hometown who decided to come here after work.

Someday, you'll be telling your grandkids about how people used to shop like this. Sounds antiquated, doesn't it, when you compare it to ordering a few things with your phone while lying on the floor with a gin and soda* resting on

....

* Gin was the first thing my best friend and I ever drank illicitly in a basement. We stole a bottle of it from her brother's mini fridge and mixed it with Crystal Light lemonade, and then were confused about why anyone would drink something that tasted like pine trees. Anyway, we got over it. If anyone ever gets their hands on a bottle of Isle of Harris gin, it tastes like daydreams and magic kelpies.

your stomach? Warehouses are for storing shit we order online. Not for shopping in.

The great thing is that the more you shop, the more the algorithms know about you. The bits and bytes know your size. They know you're looking for a small velvet coffee table in the shape of a vulva and a pair of mesh socks with oysters printed on them. It's like a little dance. The computer offers you up a little coffee table via algorithm, and when you don't click on it, it goes back to work, looking for something else you might like. Like Cinderella and her little helper birds. A movie you can stream on Disney+. Hit me up, Disney, publishing doesn't pay shit. #Disneypartner.

Digital Maximalist Tip

Block and report the bullshit. Just like in real life,
the online world is filled with fuckfaces.
Whether online or off, some people will always
be shitheads, including you, at some point, because
we all make mistakes. Rude customer service bots.
People bad at online dating etiquette or ones
with bad dick pic lighting. People with idiot takes
on every issue and shitty comments from
internet strangers. The great thing about the
internet that doesn't apply to real life,
however, is your ability to block those dickwads
and never hear from them again.
Unsubscribe. Block. Mute. Report. Bliss. In real life,
you'll still have to hide in the supermarket
when you see that friend from your high school
selling CBD pills for ferrets online. Online?
It's like she doesn't exist.

Recycle all your stuff and get paid for it

When the internet was a new thing, people would bring their old stuff into a shop where someone with the knowledge and skills would put it online to try and sell it and then take a commission. This was often done via a new site called eBay. These were called "eBay stores." Hilarious. Anyway, now we can sell our old shit online very easily. And buy other people's old shit online very easily. Which means the internet is one giant fucking glorious garage sale (boot sale if you're in England) where we're all buying and selling stuff in one infinite reusable and recyclable ecosystem.

This is nice because thanks to a few intrepid journalists, we now know that actual recycling is largely a scam—our carefully sorted bottles and cardboard are likely going to a secret landfill because China is no longer buying most of our recyclables for its own purposes, so the whole industry is sort of all for show, sadly. Everyone should still do it, because it's the best system we have. But know that trading/selling/buying/ donating your actual belongings is an amazing way to aid your shopping habit and to be part of some sort of small solution to the general shit-show that is our effect on the planet.

If you're not selling your stuff online yet, then get thee to the app store. Dig out all the knee-high boots your back can't handle any-more because you're fucking old now, and all the baby gear your kid shat on, and your ex's squash racket that makes you angry, and get ready to make some cash. There are dozens of places where buyers are clamoring for your old Portishead albums and used underwear. More so the latter, honestly. The internet is also a giant cesspool of other people's kink.

Reclaiming the kitchen

> *"The only time I really go on the internet is for recipes."*
>
> —BLAKE LIVELY

The kitchen is where our grandmothers' recipes come to die. The reality is that if we want to cook something, we fucking google it. Once we've picked one of the 14,000,100 available recipes for pulled pork or potato salad and scrolled through the 1,000-word intro about how special this online recipe is to the online recipe poster because it belonged to their grandmother, we can get to work. She's our grandmother now. Often there's a video, too, in case reading is too strenuous.

Someone's grandmother's potato salad

And if you don't have all the ingredients? Just tell your personal robot to order them, and your local Amazon-owned Whole Foods or Piggly Wiggly or Publix or Trader Joe's or Kroger or Hy-Vee or Loblaws or Zehrs* will have everything to you in a jiffy. Occasionally the algorithms will replace your cheap chuck steak with tenderloin (your robot knows when you need a little treat) or something inconvenient, but it usually works just fine.

pizza

---

* This was my local supermarket growing up, which was then replaced by a much larger anxiety-inducing supermarket that thankfully also offers online shopping and delivery. Zehrs had the best, largest, softest donuts in the world. If you ever see a Zehrs in small-town Canada, stop and get a donut. It puts every hipster donut place with their fuck-off hibiscus flavors to shame.

Or just connect your fridge

If asking your personal robot seems like kind of a hassle, delegate the shopping to your fridge. No, not your old, nonsentient fridge. Your new one that knows just what you need. So, a thing people used to do is open the fridge and look inside. And then notice what was lacking, and make a list about those lacking things, and then go to the store to get them. Now our fridges are online and their robot brains know what's missing. The fridge robots send an alert to our phones, allowing us to confirm their assessment and to replace the items whilst doing other things.

There are those who lament these technological changes, and who are nostalgic for the days when we'd spend hours in the sunlight-dappled kitchen, hand-stitched curtains flowing in the prairie light. Nostalgic for those early morning hours when we'd get up early, sweep the floors, stoke the coal fire, put the biscuits in the oven, and get the oatmeal started—but those people are wrong. That shit took forever and our ancestors dedicated much of their lives to this kind of pointless household labor, and that's why when dishwashers and electric ovens and shit were invented, women were very fucking excited. Next time you make guacamole with avocados someone brought to your door, using a recipe you got from avocado recipes dot com, give a little nod of thanks to whoever it is you give thanks to. Because old-timey kitchens were fucking nonsense and we're not going back.

The internet of things

"While on the space station I kept up with news a couple of ways—Mission Control sent daily summaries, and I would scan headlines on Google News when we had an internet connection, which was about half the time."

—CHRIS HADFIELD

In 1969, we sent a man to the moon—it was one of man's greatest technical achievements. (Speaking of aliens, women give life by birthing new people out of their bodies. I mean, hurrah for the moon, but also LOL. A baby! Women also invented life rafts, fire escapes, and syringes.) Anyway, now our astronauts have internet in space. Holy fuck, what an amazing universe. Here, let's blast you into the place where stars live, where you can take notes on life, earth, aliens, do a space walk, whatever. But for god's sake, make sure to keep up with the latest news.

Anyway, back to the internet in every object: There used to be a light fixture thing called the Clapper. You'd clap your hands and the light would go on. Clap again and it would go off. This was a while ago, but this tool was the first "connected" light bulb. It wasn't connected to the internet, of course. But it was sound activated, which was a big deal at the time, and also the commercials were hilarious.

Robot dog

Basically, the "internet of things" is a very dumb term for something that's actually pretty cool. It means shit that used to be not connected to the internet is now connected to the internet. Things like thermostats, fans, vacuum cleaners, doorbells, dog dishes, cars, alarm systems, speakers, light fixtures, curtains, etc. In short, your entire home is a robot now. No more opening your curtains by hand like a fucking chump. No more worries about someone breaking into your home to steal physical objects. Instead, they can hack into your digital home and terrorize you over the baby monitor or TV like an actual old-timey ghost. Increasing internet use in your home is easy: purchase every internet gadget immediately when it comes out and upgrade every year. Soon you'll never have to leave your bed.

Digital Maximalist Tip

The extreme digital detoxers would have all your shit be analog. *Don't get a connected doorbell! The feds are watching! Voluntary surveillance!* They'd rather the package thieves win than you simply give up your private life and allow 24/7 access to your family's comings and goings. Insanity. We can all 100 percent agree that we're happy to exchange any small measure of privacy for peace of mind. Smart coffee makers, connected refrigerators, smart mattresses (it's a thing, look it up), connected blinds, and baby monitors. The way the world is going, our houses will soon be extremely Jetsons-like in a few years, if that's a reference that still means anything. Which is great news. Connected everything is very convenient and this section will help you maximize the presence of the internet in all aspects of your house and home. Connect it all. Let the system work for you.

Around the world

Getting the fuck out of dodge has never been easier. When I was younger, we had to visit a travel agent if we wanted to go anywhere. It was usually a small storefront in a strip mall with a name like A+ Travel or Jackie's Vacations, and you'd sit in a plush little office chair and tell the nice lady where you'd like to go and when, and she'd type the info into her special giant computer that had access to all the secret airline information that the rest of us plebes didn't. It took about twenty minutes and the transaction required a lot of trust. Do not fuck up my vacation, Jackie. I do not want a forty-eight-hour layover in Newark.

The last vacation I booked via a travel agent was from London, England, to Mallorca, Spain. My friend and I were sick of the shitty grey and cold, and also our classes, so we walked in and told the man to send us somewhere warm. He told us about an all-inclusive two-star hotel on an island off the coast of Spain, where the sun, sex, and drugs were plentiful (that's what the brochure said, anyway), and he printed our itinerary and off we went. There was no way to check restaurant reviews ahead of time, which was fine because all we could afford were blocks of cheese, so we wandered around until we found the bars. The bars in Mallorca, I'm fairly certain, serve only two-for-one bootleg methanol, which was fine because we were young and so were our livers. Anyway, we didn't die. But these days, all that uncertainty is gone.

Booking a flight has never been easier—simply spend three to four hours or days online looking at different airline/hotel combos and searching for the best restaurants, bars, and sights at your destination. So that when you land, there's nothing left to chance. You've seen the social media pics. You know where to take the photo on the bridge where the bridge reflection makes the bridge look like a complete circle.

You know where to get the drink made with dry ice (if you're vacationing back in time to 2012, when those drinks were a thing) and where to pose on one leg with your giant sunhat while staring off into the distance and everyone else on the beach makes fun of you. Easy. Thanks, internet! For making travel a wonderful, homogenous experience for the masses.

4.

Be Well

"Do you remember when Fabio got hit in the face with a pigeon on the roller coaster and it broke his nose? Sometimes I feel like I'm the pigeon and the internet is Fabio's face. Actually, I don't know if I'm the pigeon, or I'm Fabio's face. Depends on the day, I guess."

—RYAN GOSLING

Gigabyte

Ryan Gosling is a treasure and, by all accounts, a very good and decent human being. Unfortunately, no matter how decent and good-looking we are, we sometimes say things that are nonsense. The point is, Fabio got hit in the face with a pigeon at an amusement park a long time ago, and because of the internet, we will never not know this fact. Anyway, a broken nose is nothing to laugh at and our health is important. And thanks to the internet, wearable technology, and connected apps, it's never been easier to keep track of our health and feel better. We can connect our babies to the internet—get alerts about how long they slept or when they pooped. We can connect ourselves to the internet—how fast we walked or ran, and how far. 30 steps today! Great job! The internet can even notice heart arrhythmias and save our lives. Not science fiction: reality. Sorry, digital minimalism. Being online is probably great for your health, in the long run.[*]

Diagnose that shit

> *"There was a time when people felt the internet was another world, but now people realise it's a tool that we use in this world."*
>
> **—TIM BERNERS-LEE**

If you're not using the internet to look up minor

---

[*] [Insert legal disclaimer here.]

ailments, book doctor appointments, and consult with your therapist, then you're doing life wrong.*

Back in the day, you'd use the old-timey telephone to call the local doctor, who would get in her buggy and come to see you in 48–100 hours, depending on how far away she lived and what the weather was like. Then the doctor would make a guess as to what was wrong, make a few suggestions, and you'd all open a few windows and boil some water and put a garlic poultice on your feet and hope for the best.

Nowadays, however, we can diagnose ourselves within seconds, often with life-threatening illnesses that will give us nightmares until we see an actual doctor. So, choose your resources wisely. The Mayo Clinic, for example, is a great resource that will reassure you the cut on your hand isn't also an incubator for a spider colony. The internet will also show you the one-in-ten-

---

* Go to a doctor for any illness or concern, obviously. The internet can give you information, but it can't cure you. Yet.

billion case where someone's cut did in fact become the birthplace of a million spiders, and now you know that, however small, the possibility is there. And that's what the internet is for, isn't it? Making yourself aware of all the possibilities. Of anything happening anywhere at any time and the possibility it could happen to you because it happened to someone else, somewhere, once. Comforting, isn't it?

Once you've realized you're a host for spiders and your body is a horror film, you can pick an appointment time online. The appointment bot will text you a confirmation, and all that's left to do is order a ride share on the day of your appointment.

There are also a billion communities online where people come together to talk productively about their allergies to Skittles and roast beef sandwiches, offer advice and support, and generally spend time with others who just get it.

Digital Maximalist Tip

Take a photo of all your ailments and store them
in a folder for easy reference. Is the mole
getting weirder? The rash getting bigger? Are
those actual bedbugs? Who's to say.
(The internet will say.) But they're all stored for
easy reference the next time you see your
doctor friend. Or your actual doctor. This also
works for hair and beauty reference.
You should always have a giant folder of hair photos
you like so your stylist can kindly humor you
when you show her a picture of J. Lo.
You're getting a haircut. Not drinking the blood
of newborn unicorns.

Meditation is better online

"Technology is teaching us to be human again."

—SIMON MAINWARING

analog tree = lame

One of the tenets of the digital detox is that it gives you time to reflect, meditate, contemplate. The implication is that you can't do these sorts of things online. Beg to fucking differ, tree huggers. There are billions of meditation apps that let you find peace—all while remaining online. In fact, being online is key. There are ones that remind you to breathe. Ones that allow you to look at some digital rain or listen to a campfire for sixty seconds at a time. Ones that show you a life-affirming quote that you can meditate on while standing in line at the post office to return a bunch of stuff you bought online. And the fact is, meditation for a few seconds while in the middle of your very busy day is a nice and realistic thing to do.

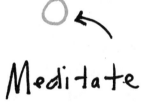

Meditate

So remember: digital detox in a Panama tree house or Italian villa = expensive and not fucking practical. One minute meditation via app? Extremely practical for like 99 percent of the population. There was something I read somewhere about that other 1 percent. What was it? Anyway, find all the meditation apps and download all of them. If you get bored after ten seconds or so, you can always swap it out for a different app. Remember, the key to meditation is instant gratification.

Tarot cards for personal growth

It used to be that getting your tarot cards read meant frequenting a small storefront in Manhattan decked out in red velvet and fake flowers, where a woman would read your palm or do your cards for twenty bucks. These places are fun and they're a part of vanishing New York that everyone is nostalgic for, but the one time I went, the woman told me my current relationship was worth fighting for and was that bitch ever wrong. Yikes. Now, luckily, you can get your cards read while you're on the toilet or pretending to listen to your new partner talk about the work commute, which was a bit hellish due to the Q not running, and if you don't like the results, just click refresh. Simple. Tarotcards.com, baby!

what's your online tarot card personality?

One of the great things about the internet is how it connects us to older traditions. Everyone loves astrology these days, for example. The sky is back in a big way, along with tarot cards, crystals, and herbal remedies. Take this quiz to find your internet tarot card destiny. Results are 100 percent guaranteed to be correct.

1. You've got which of the following apps on your phone:

 A. The one that tracks your birth time and date and tells you what energy field is affecting you at any given minute.
 B. The investment one that lets you track at what age you'll become a millionaire.

C. The one that's just an animated screen showing falling snow.

D. The one featuring endless scrolling that lets you watch fourteen-year-olds dance in sweatpants to popular music.

music

2. When you look up from your screen, your first thought is:

A. I'm fulfilling my destiny. Also, I must remember to water my virtual flower garden this afternoon.

B. Time is money and I've just wasted $47.

C. This view brings me anxiety.

D. Life is an illusion. We are all gods. We are all bits of sand and dust.

3. If you were a composite animal, you'd be

    A. a cobra made of strawberries;

    B. a dog mostly made of waterfalls but your teeth are made of gold;

    C. an aardvark made of cotton;

    D. a hummingbird made of chocolate.

dog made of
waterfalls

4. You've tried a digital detox once or twice, along with

    A. a honey enema cleanse* and throwing away all your belongings that don't bring you joy;

    B. the keto diet and microdosing;

    C. ice cream;

    D. I don't do detoxes. Depriving myself of things I actually enjoy for a small amount of time just seems sort of pointless.

....

* I made this up. Don't do this.

Your tarot card is:

Mostly As: The centaur surrounded by stars and rainbows. This coming year, you've got your head in the clouds and your brain on the internet. Not a bad combo, overall. But remember, the internet is full of nonsense and it doesn't hurt to be a bit sensible sometimes. Or not, whatever! Porcupines are aliens from the death star and cheese makes your toenails grow.

Mostly Bs: The hourglass alongside an abacus. This year, you've got goals, and those goals are related to productivity and getting shit done. The internet is a tool for you to do that, which is great. But don't forget to have fun, too. Life isn't all about the hustle. It's about the mindless passing of time, too. Do yourself a favor and do an internet search for images from the Newfoundland snowstorm of 2020. People snowboarding in the streets and drinking around neighborhood bonfires* next to seven-foot drifts will warm your heart.

....

* And filming it and putting it on the internet, obviously.

Mostly Cs: The earmuffs sitting on a sunflower. The world is a scary place and the internet is a safe space that helps you deal with that. The calming apps, the social spaces, the helpful advice—this is what you came for. Permission to be yourself. The coming year is holding you in the palm of Gwyneth Paltrow's soft, moisturized hand, which is filled with weighted blankets, mulled wine, and a vagina-scented candle.

Mostly Ds: Yarrow root and the dagger bathed in sunshine. You understand life is short and the journey long. You love letting your mind wander into the cyberworld, where everything is made of code and meaning can be found everywhere and nowhere. You've perfectly mastered the point of life and living. Which is that it's there to do whatever you want with. Online or off, life happens and how we choose to experience it is unique to us and totally fine.

Look at nature,* feel better

"The internet is so big, so powerful and pointless that for some people it is a complete substitute for life."

—ANDREW BROWN

n a t u r c

We've all heard about how we should hug more trees. Get out in nature and feel better! Look at some trees and find peace! Just go for a walk in a forest every afternoon! What's stopping you?

---

* Online, obvi.

Right, you have a job and a commute and no easy access to a fucking forest. Well guess what, motherfucks? Studies show that just *looking* at pictures of nature can reduce feelings of stress and anger. No shit! And luckily, we're online all the fucking time—with very easy access to whatever kind of nature floats our boat. A study published in *Environment and Behavior* found that college students who worked in offices with nature posters were less stressed than those in offices with no posters. Crazy, right? A picture of a tree? Reduces your blood pressure. Screenshot of a flower? Lowers your heart rate. So, set your screensavers, your lockscreen, and your home screen to a couple of trees, and boom. Relaxation unlocked. Next level.

Being offline can be dangerous to your health

In early 2020, a German woman and her friends became stranded during bad weather in the Norwegian wilderness. Her solution? Create a dating profile, obviously. Her first match was a local gentleman who also had access to a bulldozer. He showed up within five minutes of their first connection and helped clear a path to safety for her and her friends. Swoon, right? Now just imagine how fucked they'd have been without the internet on hand. And how lonely. Also hungry, probably. So the next time you get eaten by a bear on your wilderness retreat in pursuit of digital minimalism, just know that the internet could have saved you.*

A note on accessibility

> *"Oh my goodness gracious, what you can buy off the internet in terms of overhead photography. A trained ape can know an awful lot of what is going on in this world, just by punching on his mouse, for a relatively modest cost."*

> —DONALD RUMSFELD

....

* Also, always have bear spray on hand. That is a good tip from a Canadian who knows.

"We have to go see Bill Gates and a lot of different people that really understand what's happening. We have to talk to them, maybe in certain areas, closing that internet up in some way. Somebody will say, 'Oh, freedom of speech, freedom of speech.' These are foolish people. We have a lot of foolish people."

—DONALD TRUMP

Elderly people with a limited understanding of the internet and how it works can still use it to help them better participate in society, as the above quotes show. In fact, one of the things digital detoxing evangelists tend to forget is how the internet is actually essential for a huge proportion of the population—not for gaming or googling, but for general, day-to-day tasks and connections. People with accessibility issues who can't get outside easily, for example. My dad has Parkinson's disease and spends a lot of time in front of a screen—easily navigating a virtual world that's kinder to him than his real-life one that's filled with tripping hazards and impossible distances and people who can't understand him properly. Online, however, those barriers fall away. He's the same old guy. He can shop for groceries and email his friends and receive nude photos from women overseas who ask him for money, like any normal human being. He can also do his banking. People in remote communities up north can apply for jobs and video chat with grandchildren. Kids in college and university can order food to their dorms when their hangover is so strong it feels like murder. I remember once, after we had a tequila party in my dorm,* having to crawl like a sad hungover baby from my bed to the common area, where I'd stored my life-giving carton of apple juice. Nowadays, I could have just ordered a carton directly to my room like a queen or person with a butler. So remember, the digital detox is sim-

* Yes, one person left via ambulance.

ply a luxury that many can't afford—for many people, digital maximalism is the key to survival.

In short, Grandma loves her iPad so let's give her a break.

Fundraising for bullshit

Fundraising is a nice thing to do and it makes everyone involved feel good. I donated $10 to my friend's art calendar where she wears a different royal family mask while posing naked in a different state park each month. I'm such a great friend! I can't wait to hang it on my wall and make fun of it to literally anyone who asks. The internet makes it easy to do nice things like this. We're all so benevolent when it comes to online fundraising. Pat on the back, all of us.

I won't get into the fucking insanity that is fundraising for medical bills, but the internet makes it easier to help people who have been completely fucked by the US health system. This is a classic example of the government shirking its responsibilities to its citizens and requiring every unlucky family who gets fucked by an illness or accident to fend for itself. Doctors should be provided to all citizens for free by their government— just like police, firefighters, and teachers. Imagine needing police insurance before someone would come to your house after a break-in? Or fire insurance before the firefighters would help put out your house fire? Imagine everyone paying to send their kids to elementary school instead of having a system where teachers teach students for free?* Anyway. The internet allows us to contribute money or to voice support for projects like your friend's self-published book about orgasms or your friend of a friend's toenail removal or your neighbor's baked granola business.

The internet is also a good place where people can crowdsource information like, does my ballsack look weird, see pic. In the history of the world, we've never had the opinions of so many strangers at our disposal. Use this power wisely.

* I understand some people do this anyway. Sometimes when you've just got too much money, it becomes a bit of a burden and you need to get rid of it somehow.

The internet has no germs

In the olden days, if you were sick or wanted to stay healthy, you'd have to visit a shaman, a local witch, or someone else skilled in the art of herbal magix and incantations. As medical science evolved, we leaned less on magical spells and discovered the benefits of disinfectants like bleach and preventative medicines like vaccines, and our kindergarden teachers taught us the wisdom of handwashing and not touching our butts. Some stuff was still a bit of a mystery, of course. Tuberculosis? I don't know, go to the mountains for three years until your lungs feel better? Science.

Today, we still basically know nothing, but we do know a lot more than our ancestors ever did. The air can still kill us. That was a shock, eh? Invisible things wish us harm. What we know now is what to do about it: Wash your hands. Stay away from crowds. And embrace the health benefits of a life lived online. The only illness you're going to get online is perhaps a mental one—be careful out there. But honestly, apart from your actual screen (full of germs!), the internet is a virtual safe place that's free from illness and virus and bacteria. Go ahead, go out in public, online. Livestream a concert. Update your social feeds. Watch some cooking videos. Watch any livestream you like—the zoo has some good ones. It's never been easier to be social while staying safe from uncivilized people who don't care about coughing on you. Use your grimy finger to scroll in the privacy of your own home. No risk of spreading. No risk of catching. Amazing! Give thanks for this fantastic public health invention. And feel pity for our old-timey relatives who had to read books or take walks if they were sick.

5.

We're All Fucking Robots Now

"We judge on the basis of what somebody looks like, skin color, whether we think they're beautiful or not. That space on the internet allows you to converse with somebody with none of those things involved."*

—BELL HOOKS

....

* This is also why catfishing is a thing. No one knows what the fuck you look like, so why not be an up-and-coming Ukranian model stuck in Paris and needing a plane ticket to come and visit you, sweetheart! Please do not even think anything bad, I love you and will be with you soon!

Once upon a time, people met strangers by accident in the real world and decided to go on a date. That probably still happens, somewhere where the internet doesn't exist, but most people in love and getting married today probably had their first actual exchange online—whether via a wink, a "hi what's your favorite type of fossil," or a dick pic. In fact, a recent study called "Disintermediating Your Friends: How Online Dating in the United States Displaces Other Ways of Meeting," the researchers found that, basically, meeting someone online (rather than through a mutual friend) for the purposes of boning is pretty common these days. Thanks for the insight, professors! Here's some more grant money from Obvious Inc. Anyway, this is great news for most people.

One of my friends is 6'2" and blonde, and you won't be surprised to know that if she goes out in public, strangers who are physically attracted to her will approach to ask if she's free to have sex with them. For the rest of us unlikely to attract that sort of attention, the internet is a wonderful place to turn for potential love and the inevitable sadness that follows. "People who have in the past had trouble finding a potential partner benefit the most from the broader choice set provided by the dating apps," says one of the study's authors. Basically, if you're not meeting people at school, at work, or via mutual friends (i.e., if you work from home and all your friends are married), then the internet is your friend. Your only option. Your lifeline in a dating sea of shit. Good news all around!

If you do happen to somehow meet someone in real life before meeting them online: always, always, always check their social media profile as soon as possible. Just say you need the toilet and get on that phone! We all do it, so don't feel bad about it. Perhaps they seem nice, but their profile picture is them kneeling shirtless in front of a drugged-up tiger. Make your excuses, and move on.

Sleep with your phone

"The internet carries the flag of being subversive and possibly rebellious and chaotic and nihilistic."

—DAVID BOWIE

latest phone

If you're lucky, you had a slutty phase. Probably in university or college, when you realized other people's consensual bodies are fun and beer is useful. Excess is best. Ask anyone I went to university with. Multiple partners, owning more than one dog, having eggs *and* pancakes. We all like being a little bit extra sometimes, and who doesn't? Literally every person loves excess.

It's how many of us were raised. Consume, consumerism, excessive capitalism, we learned from the best—looking at you, founding fathers! But at some point, we all tend to settle down a bit. We like a bit of consistency. We want to know what to expect. Which is why we should all be sleeping with our phones. Forget your partner or your pets. Sleeping with your phone is the best (and most satisfying) relationship you'll ever have. It's always there for you. It's never mad when you wake it up at 2 a.m. to ask "what's the best arepa truck in San Diego" or what time the Banana Museum near Palm Springs opens. (Answer: Whenever the owner feels like showing up. Take your chances.) And more importantly, unlike your IRL partner, it's always listening . . .

Talk to your phone

A study at the University of Edinburgh found that people who reported their partner had become "less responsive" over the period of the study were 42 percent more likely to *die* within twenty years. The results show that perhaps if your partner is a shitty listener, it increases your own stress levels to the point where you kick it. Which brings us to our phones—the best listeners available to humankind, apart from spy satellites.

Habersham Bed.

"Hey," you say out loud to partner. "Could you not fucking crunch your pickled jalapeños so fucking loud? It's literally like tiny bombs going off in my brain and I'm going to murder you." And without fail, your phone has heard you. Minutes later, it's offering you ads for Kevlar vests, marriage therapy, and earmuffs. Thanks, phone! Once, after talking about bedroom furniture, I got an ad on my phone for a "Habersham cloister bed" that featured two single canopy beds connected by a joint headboard. It came with hanging light fixtures and a doorway at the foot of the beds and it cost $30,000. I felt heard.

But there is more to life than a cloister bed. Google has a feature that lets you reminisce to it directly. It transcribes those thoughts and keeps them for posterity. Sort of an audio diary/voluntary surveillance tool/confessional. So when you say, "Why the fuck was I dating that piece of shit?," Google will show you photos of their dog and remind you that it was mainly because of their dog. Or it can remember nice things about your mom or grandma. "Grandma loved her Pall Malls." "Mom was born in a taxi." Etc. Good and bad—all your memories are now outsourced and impossible to forget. We can all embrace old age knowing that while our soft, little organic brains are slowly shrinking, our online brain is as robust and infallible as ever.

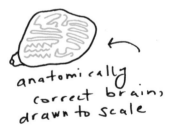

anatomically
correct brains
drawn to scale

Search bar

Our phones always know what we need. What we're searching for. What would make us complete. Studies show that active listeners make the best partners—this means when you're complaining about the temperature of your coffee or worrying about the lead levels in your water, your partner isn't interjecting, offering advice, or judging. They're simply there for you, at any time. And offering up useful responses that you're free to read or disregard at any time. So, the next time you complain about the lead levels in your water, feel comforted to know that your phone is listening—and will offer you up a few advertisements, letting you know that in places like New York, for example, the government offers free lead-testing kits to all citizens. All you have to do is get online and request one. You owe it to your health.

Porn for everyone all the time

Sexy nudie photography used to be a lovely art form amongst the pervy Victorians. Black-and-white images of ladies on lounges with massive bush. Elegant and shapely young men with moustaches and one leg atop a wooden chair. These were replaced by porn mags—*Hustler* and *Playboy*. The ones frustratingly wrapped in plastic and kept on a high shelf at the corner store. The ones your classmates would pass around and keep under their beds. Getting access to naked people used to be such a fucking hassle. Enter the internet. Responsible for a million sex educations. Especially in areas with no actual sex ed.* Porn is easily the most searched-for thing on the inter-

....

* Our sex ed in Canada was very robust. I remember watching a British cartoon in grade two that taught us all about our "naughty bits." It takes a confident school system to not only teach its tiny wards about sex, but to teach them via a sarcastic British program that in retrospect seemed like it was produced by the guys from Monty Python.

net, by a million percent.* The internet is a glo-rious repository for anything you might be into. Including suppositories. No judgment! It's all there for your private consumption. Hentai. Missionary. Doing it while wearing socks. Doing it while wearing no socks. It's a place to explore and learn and get off. These days, a lot of sex-ed classes are also teaching kids to recognize that this shit is mainly for entertainment purposes. Actual partners aren't meant to act (or look) like those on our screens. At least for now. The per-sonalized sex robots are coming (lol), and soon our online kinks will be uploaded into a soft sil-icone thing with a realistic voice that doesn't say things like, "Ow, you're on my hair," and we'll be off to the races. Robot love is on the way—and it's probably the next thing Luddites will freak out about. Anyway, until the near future when we're all fucking the sad robot version of the one that got away, take comfort in your warm little

---

* Factual.

online porn world. Relieve some stress. And be thankful you're not jerking off to a Sears catalogue like our ancestors.

magic or technology?

FOMO? More like NO MO'

Social media is bad for you, according to science. So is sitting down. Coffee. Wine. Microplastics. Flying in an airplane. New furniture (formaldehyde fumes, obvi) and literally anything else you enjoy. The worry is that when you look at other people doing things, you'll be sad you're not also doing that thing. Or if you look at other people who have photoshopped their waists and eyeballs and skin, that you'll be sad you don't also look like that photoshopped thing. The worry is that being on social media makes you sad. It's also the best.

One of the best things about being online all the fucking time is that you never miss out on anything. You're plugged into the beating robot heart of every single thing happening in your social world. Friends went on vacation without you? Watch every single one of their stories and like each of their posts. It's like you're there with them! They know it, and you know it. Didn't get to the Oscar-viewing party your work friends were having? Stream it live. You get to watch the show without all the nattering from Hans, who really thinks that Tom Hanks is overrated and that that other actor, who is seventeen and does Polish art films with subtitles, is under-appreciated. Hans really loves film and wanted to go to film school but ended up in account-ing instead, which is cool. But they're an artist at heart. Jesus fuck. Every party has one. Plus, the internet allows you to be up-to-date on the status of every person you've ever had a romantic relationship with, which is a full-time job at this point, you minx. And you'll have FOMO NO MO' when you look at what they're up to these days. Parenting. The suburbs. Or if you're younger, cocaine. Bartending. Thank god that's over, right? If you change your mind, of course, they're just a keyboard click away.

Tiny content strengthens friendships

"I really love the internet. They say chat-rooms are the trailer park of the internet . . . I find it amazing."

—CARRIE FISHER

You remember those email forwards you'd get back in the day from your sweet auntie or your dad? The ones that were like, "This is an email daisy chain. Send this to everyone you know or your true love will drown in a vat of acid." Or the ones that were just a list of rude British one-liners?* Conversing in memes (and GIFs and screenshots of the stuff acquaintances post that you need to make fun of) or broadcasting videos of yourself dancing is the new email forward. It lets your loved ones know that you're thinking of them, and that you love them, but not enough to actually compose them a personal message or to relay actual information. Thinking of you! Here's a thing where a small cat gives a large dog a massage! Here's a four-second vid of me making my eyelids look like a fox! Friends for life! And you'll stay that way, as long as you keep sending them. "Instead of small talk, we just send memes. That's how I make friends," says one teenager some-

---

* "Did you hear about the guy who died of a Viagra overdose? They couldn't close his casket." That sort of thing. I don't think email forwards are a thing anymore and thank god. They were long and pointless. Internet users have cleverly broken down these time-wasting emails into more manageable chunks. I suppose once your parents catch on and start sending you memes, it will be time to invent something new. Something smaller. Something tiny and funny, like a doodle made of the letter G that old people just don't get. Something that shows you care in a newer, more efficient way.

where, probably. And rightly so. You're busy doing lots of things these days. Look how many tabs you have open on your browser. So taking one to three seconds to text your group chat a meme is a nice way to show you care.

Digital Maximalist Tip

All holiday and New Year's cards and birthday cards and birth announcements should be sent via the internet. The great thing about e-cards is they're designed to look like actual paper. A thing no one will remember in forty years. Just like how the little "save" icon is an image of a floppy disk. Or the "erase" icon represents an actual rubber eraser. So, send a very real-looking paper e-card for every occasion. Sending cards requires a lot of fore-thought. Which we don't have anymore. Because the internet has eliminated the need for it.

GPS can save your relationship

At first glance, the development of GPS and online maps may seem an odd entry for the relationship section. However, if you're old enough to remember driving while having a screaming match with your partner or ditzy fucking friend who was supposed to be reading the analog map but fell asleep and you missed your turn on a highway and the next exit isn't for 56 miles, you'll understand the joy of the automated map. No more unreliable shotgun passenger protesting that after eight hours of map reading, they were "tired."

Basically, pre-phone and navigation systems, you had to go online and *print out* directions (remember MapQuest?). There was even an awful time before that, before the internet existed, when you needed to consult a paper map if you were visiting someplace new. Or you needed to ask someone who'd give you directions like, "You see that farmhouse up there? You take a left there, and about fifteen minutes on you'll see the sign for the 101 and you want to go south until you hit North Dakota, where you want to hang a left." And you'd promptly forget what that person said and ask someone else, who'd tell you something equally fucking confusing. Paper maps and road atlases also don't show detours, road works, real-time traffic, or any other useful shit you may need to know. They also can't talk to you. Which means pulling over to consult your analog map every few minutes, which is hard to do when you're alone and on a highway. Today our GPS can talk to us and tell us where to go. Which also means less fighting when the person who's supposed to be giving directions falls asleep or fucks it up. GPS can take us happily to any address and any place in the world, mostly. As long as you're connected to the internet and have a bit of faith. One guy famously drove straight over a roundabout in England because his GPS told him to. "Straight at the roundabout" generally means follow the roundabout around and exit accordingly, heading in the same direction you were going. Not to this guy. Straight meant over the fucking little hill. That's trusting your robot. Cheers to that guy.

send love

Relationships don't have to end: keep all your contacts forever

A digital minimalism to-do list often advocates deleting contacts from your phone. The ones you don't use very often. Which actually seems like it's creating a sort of complicated emotional task for no reason. I mean, what for? Contacts don't take up space on your phone. They're just, there. Contacts are searchable, too. So it isn't a big fucking deal to find people again if you need them. Wedding singer? Cat sitter from three years ago? Favorite restaurant that closed? Leave that shit on there. Plus, if you've ever had someone you love die, you know there's no way in hell you're deleting that number from your phone, ever. Mom is there to stay. So is Grandma and whoever else you've had the misfortune of losing. Digital nostalgia is a real thing and it's fine. Deleting shit for no reason is just busy work and another way we're made to feel shitty about the way we live life. Keep your digital relationships forever and always.

6.

Work and Finance

"One in ten thousand of us can make a tech-nological breakthrough capable of supporting all the rest. The youth of today are absolutely right in recognizing this nonsense of earning a living."

—R. BUCKMINSTER FULLER

In the classroom and on the clock, the internet is an essential tool. If this comes as a surprise to you, I congratulate you on working . . . I don't know. In a bunker? Literally every job requires the internet these days. Soybean farming in Iowa? Connected tractors with GPS and computer screens. Heritage knitting on the Shetland Islands? E-commerce website and social media. Diploma from DeVry University?* That shit's all online. So read on to learn how to maximize your internet use at work and at school.

Say yes to notifications to decrease productivity

What's the point of being online if you're not getting constant, endless updates about everything at all times? A study from the University of California, Irvine found that after a notification has distracted us from the task at hand,

....

* Did you know DeVry was founded to teach radio repair in the 1930s?

it can take about twenty-three minutes to get back on track. Sounds great, right? Everyone is so obsessed with productivity these days. And you're not some kind of worker drone just out to create more capital for your corporate overlords.

You need a distraction now and then. Take some time right now and turn on all the notifications for every app on your phone. Updates about the work commute? Yes. Calendar notifications, obviously. Notifications when your Auntie Sally uploads 147 pictures of your niece's gymnastics meet? Yes. News updates, of course. The government is completely reliable when it comes to issuing nuclear reactor meltdown or incoming missile alerts, so you want to be sure to get those. That'll give you time to retreat to your underground bunker, if you're rich, or climb into a manhole, if you're not. Welcome to the future, where you worship the rat king with all the other apocalypse refugees.

Anyway, make sure your phone is filled with

those little red notification bubbles. You have 14,035 new emails. You have 78 overdraft alerts from your bank. 801 social media updates. And the news . . . it just keeps coming. As it will until the end of time. Might as well know about it. You can get your work done later.

New jobs with a pajama dress code

With every new development in technology, there are jobs that become obsolete. With the horseless carriage came the worry that all those who worked in the stables would be out of a job. Automated rope machines mean no more work for ropemakers or shoe stitchers and whatever other old-timey jobs you can think of. Switchboard operator. Street lamp lighter. Coal delivery driver. Milkman. Travel agent. Asbestos miner.

While automated robots are definitely stealing our jobs, the internet is creating jobs, as well. A study by the US Bureau of Labor Statistics found that employment in computer and information tech jobs is projected to grow 12 percent from 2018 to 2028, much faster than any other type of occupation. Which means around half a million new jobs with a median annual wage of $86,320. Sounds better than ropemaking, right? And I'd argue that anyone nostalgic for the pre-internet era has never had the pleasure of working from home. Something that's easy to get accustomed to, under the right circumstances.

So, if you're sick of showing up to work every day dressed in "clothes" like some sort of idiot, turn your sights to one of the many new career opportunities possible thanks to the gift given to us by the internet gods: social media manager, for example. The one where some corporation wants to pay you minimum wage to manage fourteen social media platforms and to create "viral content" for them. Or jobs like virtual assistant, data scientist, podcast producer, rideshare driver, app developer, drone operator, UX designer, influencer.

You get the idea. Lose a shit ton of jobs due to tech. Gain a shit ton of jobs due to tech. Time is a flat circle. So apply now. Add a tech job to your daily routine and enjoy better energy, higher wages, and whiter teeth! And the next time your current boss wants you to pop by the office, remember, BYTE ME. Just tell them you've got it handled via Slack.

MAXIMIZE YOUR ONLINE TIME WITH THESE IMPORTANT JOBS:

1. Garage attendant

2. Toll booth operator

3. Lifeguard

4. Russian propaganda creator for Facebook

5. Camp counselor. Give all the kids forest whistles. You'll definitely find them again.

6. Freelance writer

7. Barista

8. Airplane pilot. It's mostly autopilot at this point, right?

9. Bus driver

10. Parent. All the best parents are online. How else would you be able to join a mommy/daddy group and discover that grapes are bad for babies and mothers-in-law are pieces of shit.

11. Influencer

IT'S CALLED "SLACK" FOR A REASON

....

Bosses are big into productivity tools that enable us worker bees to produce more content or automotive glass* or whatever people still make these days. Tools like Slack. A messaging service that allows anyone in your company to contact you at any time. No, no. It's not email. It's a different, bullshit thing. Slack is the modern-day water cooler. It facilitates endless distractions with side channels and sub-side channels with ever smaller groups of cooler people, which enables the most glorious shit-talking that is, indeed, very productive.

In yesteryears, if we wanted to waste time, we'd have to hang around the water cooler or next to one of those coffee pod things that every office had before we knew it killed all the turtles. No more. Thanks to work productivity tools.

....

* I mean, have you seen *American Factory*? It's glorious. We're all doomed. Thanks, Obama.

Zoom is the new meeting that could have just been an email

Pajamas
24/7

None of us ever need to attend an in-person meeting again. There is no excuse. Meetings are online now and, while they're still a giant fucking pain in the ass—why do we need to see everyone's face?—they're still a hell of a lot better than actually sitting together in a grey room with an oversized cherry veneer desk, medium-hard bagels, a tiny bottle of water, and a PowerPoint presentation that makes you want to die. That's all Zoom now. Sit in your shitty little eat-in kitchen, pick a chic virtual background that makes it look like you've got your shit together and didn't get up 40 seconds ago, and click that link to join. Pretend you're happy to see everyone and do that dumb Muppet wave whenever someone new joins the conference. Wardrobes are business on top and party on the bottom. If you're hungover or hating life or you just forgot because time has no meaning when you're working from home, you can have a technical issue—sorry guys! 2020 is the year in-person meetings were laid to rest. It remains true that every meeting, virtual or not, is a waste of time. Feel an urge to schedule a meeting? Do not. Send a group email instead and respect everyone's fucking time. We'll all get there someday.

Online banking is the shit

"If you count email, I'm on the internet all day, every day."

—BILL GATES

banking

One of the world's richest people is online all the fucking time. If you care about things like unmitigated wealth and if you admire that, or if you aspire to obtain the sort of wealth that lets you buy a pet cheetah or an island made of gold, then it would be best to follow his lead and get online.

Anyway, remember going to the bank and bringing your little bank book and then filling out little slips of paper that said "deposit" or "withdrawal"? And you'd write in your account number and the bank teller would update your little bank book with their old-school printer to reflect your new balance? And then you'd get in your car and go about doing all those other in-person errands that are pointless and take forever—grocery shopping, doctor's appointments, vet visits? If not, you're lucky and also very young.

Anyway, a young woman who was cat sitting for us recently saw a book of checks on our table, and her disgust was palpable. "I didn't know people still used checks," she said. Old age is coming for all of us. I take comfort in the fact that this young cat sitter will eventually be confused by some sort of advanced technology when she hits the age of thirty.

Anyway, as we all know, banking is now online. Transfer money, deposit checks, send $5 to your friends to pay for the tangerines, pay the phone bill, freak out over your nonexistent balance and/or life savings or your debt.

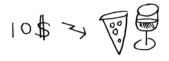

Chargers: own forty and charge everywhere

My final bit of advice in this book is perhaps the most valuable. Do not forget this: Our electrical devices are fallible. They require charging every so often, which is a bit of a pain. I assume the tech bros and lady are working on devices that charge via CO_2 emissions or via Patagonia fleece. Until the technology catches up to our needs, you should own multiple chargers and power bars so you're never without a cord.

Bedroom. Bathroom. Car. Purse. Charger. Preferably one right by your bed, so when you wake up, everything is at 100 percent including your delightful, well-rested body, you badass. Looking good! Is there an app for that? A little voice that tells you how lovely you are whenever you look at a screen? Or one that pipes up to mitigate how you feel after reading a negative comment online. "The climate crisis is real and you're

all still using plastic bags, you pieces of shit," followed by a little voice that goes, "Yeah, but your
eyebrows look really good today. Take heart, little
human. We're all doing our best." I'd download
that app. Anyway, be sure everything is charged
at all times, and the only way to do that is to have
a zillion chargers everywhere you roam.

in conclusion

"The internet is part of this ongoing, species-long project we've been working on since we climbed down out of the trees in the savanna. We've been working on it without really knowing it."

—WILLIAM GIBSON

Look, screens have won. We all know it now. They're essential, beautiful, and probably a bit magic—no one really knows, really. Science is just a thing people choose to believe in or not, right?* Anyway, the myth of digital minimalism

* This was aimed at Gwyneth but, in reality, she seems very fun and someone you'd want to drink wine with. So, live and let live.

153

has been destroyed. Destroy is a strong word, but this is a book full of strong words. Cock. Science. Iodide. I hope it's been a joyful, informative journey and that you're feeling a bit better about your rampant, irresponsible internet use that has changed your brain. The next time someone tells you to get offline, take a walk, try a digital detox, tell them your brain is wired for the internet now and it's all good. You're an advanced being. A supertasker. Your life is in the cloud. And you've never felt better. Or just tell them to fuck off. Judgmental fucking cocks. It's the age of the internet. And it's up to us to take advantage of it. Go send a meme to everyone in your contact list. Because eighty years ago, your grandparents had no dishwasher and had to go to the grocery store on a horse. You owe it to Granny, really. Live the life of excess that humankind has earned after a long, hard slog through a world without tech and full of tuberculosis and cars that don't even speak to you. Life is short. Get the fuck online. And tell someone you love them.

emergency offline checklist

In the unlikely event that you're somewhere without access to the internet (on a clifftop, underwater, mid-apocalypse, etc.), here are some emergency activities to pass the time until you can get online again. The important thing is not to panic. Try to remember how many open tabs you had on your laptop, then count those while breathing deeply through your nose. Repeat. And try out some of these offline time-wasters.

❏ Try some analog "face time" with your partner or children

❏ Dog ear book pages or underline your favorite passages

❏ Hand wash your delicates

- ❑ Buy shampoo at your local pharmacy
- ❑ Play a board game
- ❑ Wait in line
- ❑ Draw designs all over your hands and arms
- ❑ Wake up and lie there for a bit
- ❑ Make a little bonfire out of important papers you've already stored in the cloud
- ❑ Walk through leaves
- ❑ Swim in a pool or ocean
- ❑ Peel the price tag from something and get it stuck under your fingernails
- ❑ Sit in a hot tub
- ❑ Ride the bus and look out the window
- ❑ Get shitfaced with your friends
- ❑ Wash dishes
- ❑ Listen to actual records
- ❑ Pet a cat or dog
- ❑ Say hello to wildlife
- ❑ Masturbate with a non-battery-operated device

- [ ] Take a pottery class
- [ ] Water a plant
- [ ] Go to the theater
- [ ] Rake leaves
- [ ] Mash potatoes
- [ ] Paint your toenails
- [ ] Get a blister and complain about it
- [ ] Ask someone for directions
- [ ] Tell the barista how nice it is outside
- [ ] Any weather-related conversation, really
- [ ] God. That was fucking horrible. I'm so sorry. Hopefully the emergency has passed and you have recovered from your brief foray into analog life.

reading list

There's a reason books about the internet, the digital world, are fantastical, full of possibilities, and mostly science fiction. The internet holds so much potential, it's hard to process how it's affected us and all the possibilities the future holds for us. Immortality. Flying cars. Connected coffee makers. The list is endless. So if you're enjoying this book and sick of reading about how the internet and your phone are the downfall of humanity, here are some reading recommendations to make you feel better.

Snow Crash by Neal Stephenson

Credited with the first appearance of the word "avatar" to mean digital likeness, this is a sprawling maniacal read about the mafia, pizza delivery, and the end of the world in a dystopian Los Angeles. It's very badass.

Ready Player One by Ernest Cline

Video games, '90s culture, Furbies, probably, I can't remember at this point, I read it a while ago, and one major quest.

Neuromancer by William Gibson

This is the gold standard of science fiction and everyone should read it.

The Left Hand of Darkness by Ursula K. Le Guin

Feminist science fiction set in a fantastical world where "mindspeak" is the thing. Who needs talking out loud when you can communicate brain to brain, right?

acknowledgments

Thanks to my editor Ann Treistman, copyeditor Ashley Patrick, book designer Nick Caruso, and everyone at The Countryman Press who helps make books like this a success. Thanks to Euan Thorneycroft, my agent at A. M. Heath. Thanks to Al Gore for inventing the internet.